**Date: 2/3/12**

# GIRAFFES

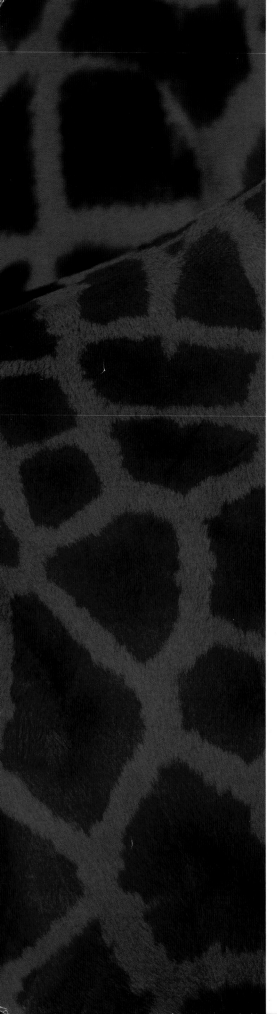

## LIVING WILD

Published by Creative Education

P.O. Box 227, Mankato, Minnesota 56002

Creative Education is an imprint of The Creative Company

Design and production by Mary Herrmann

Art direction by Rita Marshall

Printed in the United States of America

Photographs by Dreamstime (Jenny, Pemotret, Sloth92), Shen Du, Getty Images (Adrian Bailey/Aurora, Central Press/Hulton Archive, Richard Du Toit, Suzi, Eszterhas, DAVID HECKER/AFP, Gerald Hinde, Beverly Joubert, George F. Mobley/National Geographic, Steve & Ann Toon, Art Wolfe, ZSSD), iStockphoto (Kitch Bain, Hendrick De Bruyne, Julianne DiBlasi, Dirk Freder, Steve Geer, Patrick Gijsbers, David T Gomez, Dennis Guyitt, Hazlan Abdul Hakim, Emin Kuliyev, Peter Malsbury, Eli Mordechai, David Olah, Diane Peacock, Thomas Polen, Brandon Seidel, Nico Smit, Eliza Snow, Rick Wylie, Lisa Young)

Library of Congress Cataloging-in-Publication Data

Helget, Nicole Lea.

Giraffes / by Nicole Helget.

p. cm. — (Living wild)

Includes index.

ISBN 978-1-58341-654-9

1. Giraffe—Juvenile literature. I. Title. II. Series.

QL737.U56H45 2008

599.638—dc22    2007014996

CPSIA: 032511 PO1440

9 8 7 6 5 4 3

🍎 CREATIVE EDUCATION

# GIRAFFES

Nicole Helget

The orange sun beats down on the dry

grasslands of Zimbabwe. A herd

of female giraffes, along with their young
calves, gathers to drink water from the river.

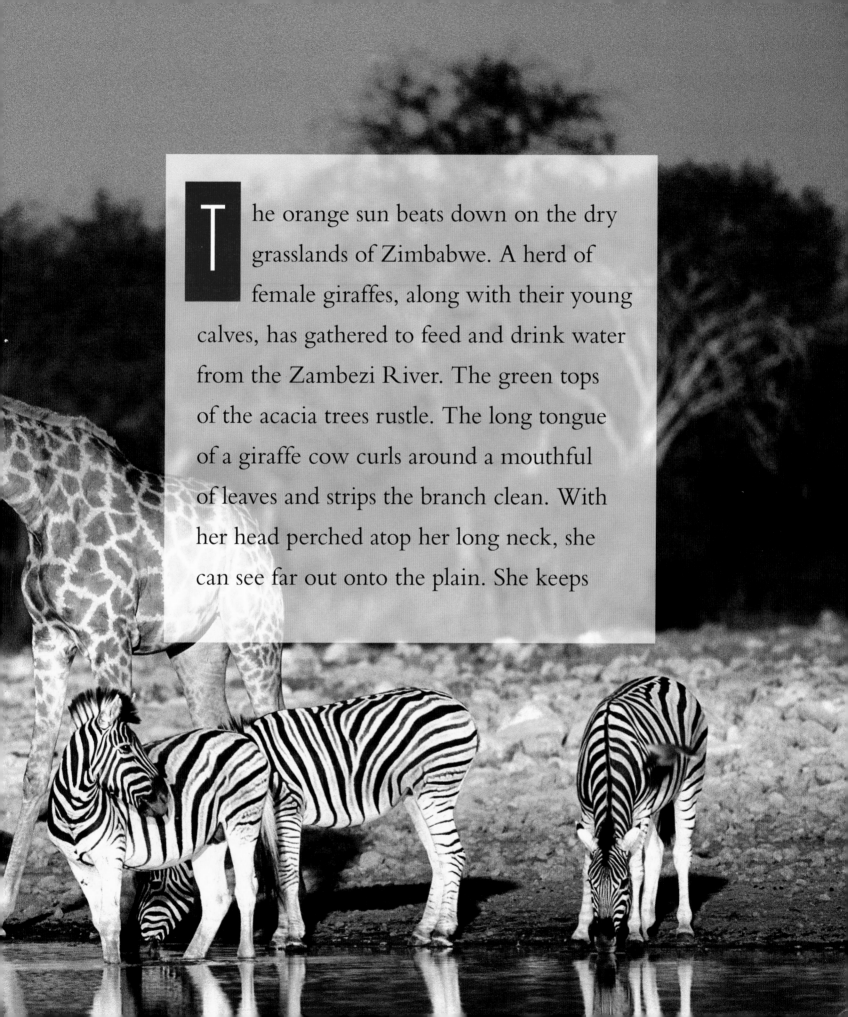

The orange sun beats down on the dry grasslands of Zimbabwe. A herd of female giraffes, along with their young calves, has gathered to feed and drink water from the Zambezi River. The green tops of the acacia trees rustle. The long tongue of a giraffe cow curls around a mouthful of leaves and strips the branch clean. With her head perched atop her long neck, she can see far out onto the plain. She keeps

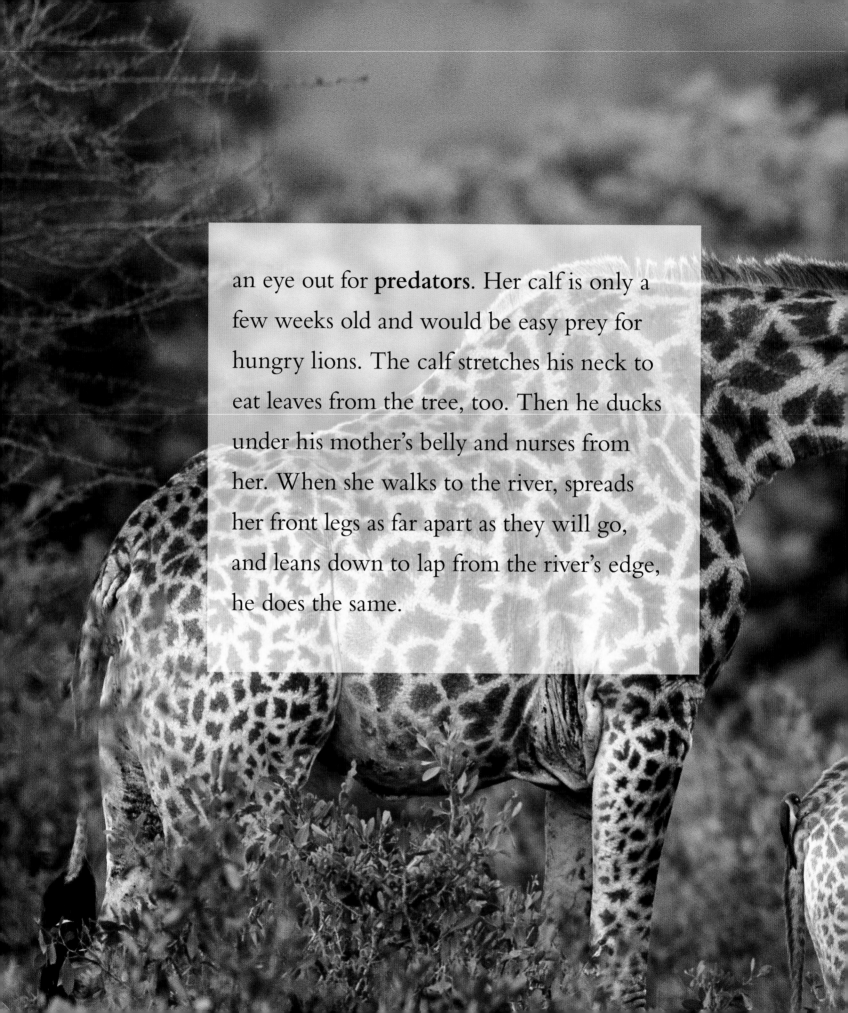

an eye out for **predators**. Her calf is only a
few weeks old and would be easy prey for
hungry lions. The calf stretches his neck to
eat leaves from the tree, too. Then he ducks
under his mother's belly and nurses from
her. When she walks to the river, spreads
her front legs as far apart as they will go,
and leans down to lap from the river's edge,
he does the same.

# WHERE IN THE WORLD THEY LIVE

☐ **Somali (or Reticulated) Giraffe**
Somalia and Kenya

☐ **Angolan (or Smoky) Giraffe**
Angola and Zambia

☐ **Kordofan Giraffe**
western and southwestern Sudan

■ **Masai (or Kilimanjaro) Giraffe**
central and southern Kenya and Tanzania

■ **Nubian Giraffe**
eastern Sudan and north-eastern Congo

☐ **Rothschild Giraffe**
Uganda and north-central Kenya

■ **South African Giraffe**
South Africa, Namibia, Botswana, Zimbabwe, and Mozambique

☐ **Thornicroft (or Rhodesian) Giraffe**
eastern Zambia

☐ **West African (or Nigerian) Giraffe**
Niger and Cameroon

Giraffes are native only to the continent of Africa. The single species of giraffe is divided into nine subspecies, based on the different colorations of giraffes found in various parts of Africa. The colored dots represent the home territories of each subspecies.

## SENTINELS OF THE SAVANNA

*The distinctively marked and solitary okapi was not discovered by modern scientists until 1900.*

A giraffe's lanky body is perfectly designed for life on the hot African **savanna**. Its great height is an advantage when **foraging** for leaves or watching for predators, and its tall and long shape allows for even distribution of the sun's powerful rays, leaving the giraffe relatively cool.

Giraffes belong to the family Giraffidae. Their closest relative is the zebra-like okapi, the only other member of the Giraffidae family. Giraffes were once thought to have descended from camels and leopards, a belief reflected in their scientific name, *Giraffa camelopardalis*. *Giraffa* comes from an Arabic word that has several different meanings, including "one who walks swiftly," "creature of grace," "lovely one," and "tallest of all mammals."

The unique shape and color of the giraffe make it one of the most easily recognizable animals on the planet. Giraffes typically have buff-colored bodies with darker brown spots of various shapes, sizes, and patterns. The giraffe's spots can be pale yellow to black, including different shades of brown, while its background color can range from white to light brown. A giraffe's spot patterns

*Giraffes work together and live in groups; females and males stay in separate groups most of the time.*

and coloring depend upon where it lives. Giraffes rarely travel far, so they mate with other giraffes in their area, passing along the jagged, leafy, or blotched spot patterns to their young. This keeps alike-spotted giraffes in the same general areas.

The giraffe is the tallest of all land-living animals. Male giraffes, called bulls, can be 18 feet (5.5 m) tall and weigh up to 3,000 pounds (1,360 kg). Females, or cows, are generally slightly shorter and lighter than males. The giraffe's body gently slopes from the shoulder to the rump. This slant helps distribute the pressure caused by carrying such a heavy neck. The slight hump near the giraffe's shoulders contains the muscles that hold up and control its most distinctive feature—the neck.

The giraffe's five- to six-foot (1.5–1.8 m) neck is made up of seven **vertebrae**, just like other mammals. But the giraffe's neck bones and muscles are much larger, to accommodate the longer neck. An extended windpipe runs from the mouth and nose to the giraffe's extra-large lungs. The lungs need to be especially powerful to force air in and out through the long length of the giraffe's neck. The giraffe's heart is also exceptionally big—

Animals such as giraffes and monkeys do not seem to mind the roads humans have made in their habitats.

*Tick birds may be pesky, but they also eat harmful bugs and ticks.*

Tick birds are pests to giraffes. They peck giraffes' sores and eat their blood and bits of flesh. They even pluck giraffes' hair for nests.

weighing up to 25 pounds (11.4 kg)—so that it can pump blood up the neck to the head.

Giraffes are **ruminants**; between feedings they chew their "cud," or food. Instead of upper incisor teeth, giraffes have only gum pads with which to chew. A giraffe has a four-chambered stomach. After a giraffe eats, the food makes its way through two chambers, then the cud is **regurgitated** into the giraffe's mouth, where it is chewed and mixed with saliva to help aid digestion. The cud is swallowed again and then travels through the remaining two chambers.

A giraffe has two types of **gait**. One, called pacing, is slow. The giraffe carefully moves the legs on one side of its body forward, then brings the other side's legs forward. Scientists speculate that the reason giraffes don't use a diagonal walk (where opposite limbs move forward at the same time) as other four-legged creatures do is that their legs are too long and could become entangled. When pacing, the giraffe's neck slowly moves back and forth to help maintain balance.

The giraffe's faster gait is called a gallop. While galloping, a giraffe's neck thrusts forward and backward

with greater speed. The giraffe's hind legs push off the ground together, thrusting the forelegs forward and into the air. When the forelegs touch the ground, they quickly push off again. For a brief moment, the entire body of the giraffe is airborne. Then the hind legs land together, and the process starts over. A galloping giraffe can reach speeds as fast as 40 miles (64 km) per hour.

A giraffe can also jump, clearing heights of up to five feet (1.5 m). This capability is important, now that many cattle fences have been built in Africa. The neck helps

*Even when giraffes are running at a gallop, their large eyes enable them to see everything clearly.*

*Giraffes can rest in various positions, but it is most difficult for them to stand up from lying down.*

propel the giraffe over obstacles. To jump, the giraffe first pulls its neck back, putting most of its weight over the hind legs. Then it thrusts the neck forward, lifts its front legs, and pushes off with its hind legs.

To rest, a giraffe lowers its head, sags its neck, and sometimes leans against a tree trunk. If a giraffe feels particularly safe from predators, it will lie down. To do so, a giraffe kneels on its forelegs before lowering the rest of its body onto the ground. A giraffe sleeps for only a few minutes at a time several times a night. During sleep, the giraffe rests its head alongside its body. To get back up, a giraffe uses its neck to help thrust itself onto its knees, raise its hindquarters, and straighten its back legs. Then it can straighten its forelegs and stand up.

The **habitat** of the giraffe extends throughout central and southern Africa, but most giraffes live in the areas far south of the Sahara Desert. Northern Africa today does not grow the type of **vegetation** giraffes eat, and it is too heavily populated by people. Giraffes can thrive in many climates, but they do not live in deserts or rainforests. The distribution of giraffes in Africa depends mainly on the types of vegetation present. Where acacia trees are

A giraffe can live a couple of months without drinking water if there are enough acacia leaves for it to eat. These leaves contain water.

A giraffe's tongue and mouth are specially adapted to withstand eating leaves from thorny acacia trees.

abundant, many giraffes will live, since acacia leaves are their favorite form of food.

The area where a herd of giraffes lives is called the home range. The average giraffe's home range covers 40 to 50 square miles (104–130 sq km). Giraffes walk slowly in their home range. They browse the bushes and trees for leaves to eat. There is typically a watering hole close

by, but giraffes are less dependent upon water than other animals because they get most of their water from eating the moist acacia leaves. When a giraffe does need extra water, it carefully wanders to the watering hole. It looks around for predators such as lions before going to the rim to drink, splaying its long front legs and bending its long neck to lap.

*Young giraffes (pictured and opposite) require the protection of their mothers.*

Since giraffes do not have a set mating schedule, they can give birth at any time of year. After 14 or 15 months of developing in its mother's womb, a baby giraffe, called a calf, is born. If it is healthy and not attacked by predators, it will stand in fewer than 15 minutes and **suckle** from its mother soon after. Very quickly, it will become part of the giraffe herd and begin carving out its role among the family. The baby giraffe's spots and background color are paler than adults' but will darken with age, **camouflaging** the young animal from predators such as lions.

At birth, a giraffe calf stands almost six feet (1.8 m) tall from the tip of its hooves to the top of its head and weighs between 100 and 150 pounds (45–65 kg). Its horns lay flat against its head. Tufts of black fur top the horns, which will slowly stand up over the next few months as bone replaces **cartilage**. In the first year of life, a giraffe calf adds three feet (.9 m) to its height. The calf will continue to grow taller until it is four years old. At that point, a giraffe is considered an adult and can fend for itself.

**When a mother giraffe gives birth, other females in the herd sometimes form a circle around her; they greet the newborn with nuzzles and licking.**

*Giraffes may come upon chameleons, which live in trees in Africa, while they are eating leaves.*

However, for the first few days of its life, the calf will follow its mother. (The father does not help raise his young and has little to no contact with his offspring.) The unsteady calf will test out its legs and begin prancing and galloping in its mother's shadow. After that, its curiosity will bid it to explore its world. It will smell the thorn bushes and acacia trees. It will lick chameleons and chase ostriches. Tick birds will land on its head and neck. The giraffe calf will carry them sometimes; at other times, it will shake its head and whip its neck violently to rid itself of the birds. When tired, it will flop down among the tall grasses and rest. Young calves wander together in small groups playing, nipping, and nuzzling each other, while one or two adult giraffes keep careful watch. The calves' relationship with their mothers is relaxed. Only when they are hungry will they seek their mothers to nurse from them. They will do so until they are almost one year old.

During its first year of life, a giraffe calf is susceptible to predators such as lions and hyenas. More than half of all calves born do not survive the first year. The lucky half can expect to live between 15 and 20 years in the wild. Giraffes born in zoos can live a few years longer.

In the wild, adult giraffes are not as vulnerable to predator attacks as are smaller animals such as zebras and antelope. Although the meaty giraffe can feed a **pride** of about a dozen lions for three days, bringing one down is no easy feat. Giraffes can often see lions approaching and run away before the cats can attack. If a giraffe is killed, it usually happens near a watering hole. The lions wait and stalk the animal in the cover of bushes and grass and then take advantage of the giraffe's unsteady posture while drinking to surprise it. But even then, one swift kick can

*Sometimes a giraffe will lick the bark of trees that produce a sticky, sweet substance called sap.*

A giraffe's main method of showing aggression is necking, which sometimes looks affectionate.

throw a lion or kill it instantly. Giraffes have long, muscular legs and sharp hooves.

A giraffe uses its long neck to express emotions. When angered, the giraffe lowers its neck horizontally to the ground, threatening the offending animal. To show **submission**, a giraffe extends its neck fully and points its nose in the air. Male giraffes **neck** or **spar** to determine dominance in the herd. In necking, one bull presses its shoulders against the other, swings its neck, and rams it into the other giraffe's neck. Then the two push their necks into one another in an effort to throw each other off balance and prove their strength. This behavior will continue until one of the males either concedes and wanders away or sparring results.

Sparring occurs when the giraffes take turns head slamming each other by swinging their necks and jabbing their horns into the other's neck. Soon, the head slamming disturbs the rigid posture of the giraffes, and they receive blows all over their bodies—on their backs, flanks, and shoulders. Giraffes can deliver powerful sparring blows. A warden from Kruger National Park in Africa once reported that a large bull giraffe lay

When a male giraffe has been defeated by another male, he runs away to find a new herd.

Sometimes, bull giraffes will join elephant herds. The elephants seem to benefit from the giraffe's high vantage point over the savanna.

*In the dry season when leaves are more scarce, giraffes will visit a watering hole every three days.*

unconscious for 20 minutes after being hit while sparring.

Apart from being dangerous to themselves, giraffes' main predators include leopards, hyenas, wild dogs, and crocodiles. Any of these animals may take advantage of giraffes while their legs are splayed during drinking or may attack newborn calves. Giraffes sometimes fall victim to deadly snakes as well. A Kenyan game warden once reported coming upon a dead giraffe lying on top of a dead python. Apparently, the python had wrapped itself around the giraffe's neck, which strangled it. The giraffe then fell on top of the python, crushing the snake.

Other factors that threaten the lives of giraffes include **parasites**, disease, and injuries. Fifteen different types of ticks feed on the blood of giraffes. A giraffe's intestines can host such parasites as flukes, tapeworms, and whipworms, which feed on the contents of the giraffe's intestines and can cause sickness and even death. Rinderpest, an infectious viral disease spread by air and close contact, is typically found in cattle but can pass to giraffes. It causes blindness and therefore makes animals susceptible to predators. In 1960, this disease wiped out 40 percent of the giraffe population in northern Kenya.

But of all the predators on the planet, the ones that threaten giraffes the most are humans. During World War I (1914–18), both the German and British armies constructed telephone and telegraph wires across the plains of Africa. Galloping giraffes collided with the thin wires and were injured. These wounds sometimes left the giraffes vulnerable to infection and death. Big-game hunters **decimated** the giraffe population in the early 1900s by shooting giraffes for trophies in their collections.

*The young of giraffe predators such as lions get to eat only after the adults have had their fill.*

The West African country of Namibia contains some of the oldest rock drawings featuring giraffes.

## GIRAFFES AROUND THE WORLD

Few animals enchant people so quickly as the giraffe, with its exotic characteristics, graceful gait, and peaceful disposition. As early as 2500 B.C., giraffes were captured in regions south of Africa's Sahara Desert, herded onto rafts, and floated down the Nile River toward Egypt, where they were paraded for all the people to enjoy. When pharaohs and queens of Egypt meant to enter into political relationships with other regions, a giraffe was often the gift of choice to woo leaders from other lands.

In Alexandria, Egypt, Pharaoh Ptolemy II organized an elaborate parade in about 280 B.C. The parade included 24 chariots drawn by 96 elephants, 7 chariots pulled by 14 antelope, 12 camels, 2,400 slaves each leading a hound, 24 oryx (a type of antelope), 24 lions, 16 cheetahs, 4 lynxes with their cubs, and a single giraffe. Roman dictator Julius Caesar brought the first giraffe to Rome, Italy, in 46 B.C. for his zoo. He called it a "cameleopard" because it was as tall as a camel and had spots like a leopard. Upon hearing of the creature, the citizens of Rome imagined the large creature would be as fierce as a

**In Tanzania's Tarangire National Park, a white giraffe was photographed in 2005. Rumors of the creature's existence had been heard since 1993.**

Giraffes appear to be calm and quiet most of the time.

More than 3,000 years ago, the Egyptian boy king Tutankhamen received a giraffe tail as one of his **coronation** gifts.

leopard, too. When the giraffe arrived, it did nothing but stand and gaze upon the crowd. Roman author Pliny the Elder described it as being "quiet as a sheep." For people who were used to the excitement of lions and gladiators fighting to the death in the Roman Coliseum, the calm giraffe was surely a disappointment.

It is unsurprising, then, that as the great empires of Rome and Egypt fell into decline, the giraffe population died out in Europe. Giraffes even became uncommon in Egypt, except in stories and dreams. If someone dreamed of a giraffe, Egyptians believed it meant that something bad was going to happen.

Eventually, as centuries passed and travel became easier, the giraffe again appeared in regions of the world where it was not native. In A.D. 1414, the first giraffe was brought to China along with precious stones, Arabian horses, and spices. The Chinese thought it looked like a mythical creature they called a *qilin* (*CHEE-lin*). England bought its first giraffe in 1805 for 1,000 pounds. Unfortunately, the animal died three weeks later. In Paris, France, a giraffe was added to the city zoo in 1826. It created so much excitement that women's fashion soon adopted the

*In the 15th century, Chinese artist and poet Shen Du painted this picture of the first giraffe to live in China.*

# QILIN

In the corner of the western seas, in the stagnant waters of a great morass,

Truly was produced a qilin (ch'i-lin), whose shape was as high as fifteen feet.

With the body of a deer and the tail of an ox, and a fleshy, boneless horn,

With luminous spots like a red cloud or purple mist.

Its hoofs do not tread on living beings and in its wanderings it carefully selects its ground.

It walks in stately fashion and in its every motion it observes a rhythm,

Its harmonious voice sounds like a bell or a musical tube.

Gentle is this animal, that has in antiquity been seen but once,

The manifestation of its divine spirit rises up to heaven's abode.

*Shen Du (1357–1434)*

giraffe's spots. Dresses, bonnets, gloves, and coats appeared in the familiar buff color with brown blotches. So did household items such as curtains, blankets, and napkins.

In their travels to Africa, big-game hunters in the 19th and 20th centuries sought giraffes—as well as lions, water buffalo, and leopards—for their private collections. These people hunted the animal almost to the brink of **extinction**. In countries such as Sudan, Ethiopia, and Kenya, African men had long hunted giraffes for their meat, hides, and tails. After eating the meat, the people ground the giraffe bones into small pieces, which were used as fertilizer. The tendons proved useful as guitar strings, bowstrings, or as thread for sewing. Giraffe hides were fashioned into pots, buckets, drum coverings, and shields. The tails of giraffes were used as fly swatters or ornaments. Some African tribes believed the tail of a giraffe would bring them good luck and protect them from evil spirits, so they wore them as necklaces or bracelets. Never, though, were giraffes killed at a rate that threatened their survival as a species until white people came to Africa.

The methods of the white hunters in the late 1800s and early 1900s were so effective that one European

living in Africa wrote, "This wonderful and harmless animal is being completely annihilated!" The white people used horses to run the giraffes down and exhaust

*Some wealthy people kept personal zoos of African animals.*

them, making them easier to shoot. One hunter could shoot four giraffes in 15 minutes using this method. Some giraffes were then stuffed and mounted. Others were decapitated and only their heads hung in the hunters' lodges. Some hunters stripped the giraffes of their hides and left the carcasses for the scavenging animals of the savanna. Giraffes in eastern Africa were nearly wiped out by the beginning of the 20th century.

By 1930, African countries began requiring hunters to get licenses for the privilege of shooting a giraffe. The countries issued only a few licenses each year to ensure that the giraffe population had time to regenerate. Ernest Hemingway, a popular American author, spent time on safari in Kenya observing the giraffe and hunting other big game in 1933 and 1954. Struck by the beauty of the giraffe and the land in general, Hemingway later remarked, "All I wanted to do was get back to Kenya."

In 1933, the Conference for the Protection of the Fauna and Flora of Africa was held in London, England. One of its goals was to create game reserves for the animals of Africa, including the giraffe. These reserves became places where animals could live in the wild without the threat of hunters. Now there are hundreds of game reserves throughout Africa where tourists can still go on safari. Most travel with cameras rather than guns. The money generated from these safaris helps the professionals at the game reserves monitor and care for the animals. These educated and experienced people keep track of the giraffes' health, diet, and reproduction rates.

All over the world, giraffes live in zoos where zookeepers, veterinarians, and other caretakers feed, exercise, and treat the animals. New York City's Central Park Zoo is one of the settings of the 2005 animated film *Madagascar*. A giraffe named Melman lives in the zoo and exhausts the resources of veterinarians. A hypochondriac, Melman always believes that there is something wrong with him, and he takes medicine for every possible symptom.

On May 5, 2007, people were introduced to a real baby giraffe. The calf was born at Roger Williams Park Zoo in Providence, Rhode Island. The entire birth was videotaped and uploaded to the Internet so that people from all over the world could watch the calf take its first breath and first steps.

*The process of relocating a giraffe is not a pleasant one for the animal, which is roped, tripped, and blindfolded.*

## SILENT NO MORE

Since scientists first began studying giraffes, they have worked to discover how giraffes have adapted to their changing environments. One study that may help more people become interested in preserving the giraffe is being conducted in the United States by researchers studying the communication strategies of giraffes. Another study, long and ongoing, delves into the physical function of the giraffe's long neck.

For centuries, people believed that giraffes were mute, or that they could not make sound come from their throats and mouths as other animals can. Giraffes were thought to communicate through certain swishes of their tails, by striking certain postures, or by stamping their hooves. They were known as the "silent sentinels of the savannas."

Rarely have humans recorded hearing sounds coming from giraffes. Zookeepers once heard an arthritic giraffe emit a gentle "moo" when it was being raised to its feet, presumably because it was in pain. Another zookeeper described hearing a giraffe "growl" at several calves that were trying to suckle from her. A warden at an African game reserve recalled hearing a sleeping giraffe "snore,"

In the wild, an adult giraffe eats about 74 pounds (34 kg) of leaves a day. In captivity, giraffes are fed grains and alfalfa.

and a biologist once reported being "snorted" at by a bull giraffe that seemed to be angry with him.

Recently, scientists have discovered that giraffes may be communicating with one another more often than first thought. Using highly sensitive microphones and special computer technology that measures and records sound waves, scientists have learned that giraffes may be using the same type of low-frequency sounds that whales and elephants use to communicate.

The low-frequency sounds are called infrasound waves. They travel farther than higher-pitched waves through the air, so giraffes, even when more than a mile (1.6 km) apart, can communicate. Because sorting out these infrasounds from other sounds in the wild is extremely difficult, most of the studies involving giraffe communication occur in zoos, where the animals and outside noises can be more controlled.

In 1998, researcher Elizabeth von Muggenthaler became curious about the communication techniques of the giraffe after having studied its closest relative, the okapi. Muggenthaler studied 11 giraffes in two zoos in North Carolina and South Carolina. She observed how

*Giraffes at New York's Bronx Zoo appear to be chatting as they munch on leaves.*

*Giraffes are constantly perceptive to their environment, listening for the subtle sounds of their herd members.*

sociable giraffes were, how they could be susceptible to predators, and how important it was for them to protect their young. Therefore, it seemed likely that they were communicating with one another in some way. Since giraffes had previously been considered mute, Muggenthaler thought she would take a closer look at their behavior.

Researchers working with Muggenthaler concluded that the emission of infrasounds seemed to coincide with two behaviors in giraffes. When a giraffe stretched its neck back over its body and then threw its head, lowering and raising its chin, it emitted infrasound waves. Researchers could also tell when giraffes were using infrasound by watching their ears. When one giraffe was emitting sounds, other giraffes would pert their ears, as if they were listening to something.

Another study involving giraffes has been ongoing since the study of animals became a serious matter for scientists and **naturalists** to consider. Since the early 1800s, humans have speculated and written about the biological function of the giraffe's long neck. Many have created theories that suggest that a giraffe's long neck helps it reach food. Few people have challenged this theory, but today, the debate has been renewed.

In 1809, French naturalist Jean-Baptiste Lamarck published a paper that explained the **evolution** of the giraffe's long neck. He wrote that "this animal, the tallest of the mammals, is known to live in the interior of Africa in places where the soil is nearly always arid and barren, so that it is obliged to browse on the leaves of trees and to make constant efforts to reach them. From this habit long maintained in all its race, it has resulted that the animal's forelegs have become longer than its hind-legs, and that its neck is lengthened to such a degree that the giraffe, without standing up on its hind-legs, attains a height of six meters."

Sixty years later, the famous biologist Charles Darwin expressed a similar opinion in *Origin of the Species.* He wrote, "The giraffe, by its lofty stature, much elongated neck, fore-legs, head and tongue, has its whole frame beautifully adapted for browsing on the higher branches of trees." Darwin also suggested that the giraffe's long neck helped it see great distances, giving the giraffe an advantage over stalking predators. Most people have accepted these explanations without question. But some

*A giraffe's knobby head, complete with horns, is thought to be an effective weapon against others.*

**Scientists think that giraffes are able to see in color. Some colors they seem to recognize are red-orange, yellow-green, purple, green, and blue.**

biologists now wonder whether such theories as Darwin and Lamarck's are justified.

One American biologist, Craig Holdrege, the director of The Nature Institute in Ghent, New York, questions the validity of the "food-reaching" theory. He argues that close study of giraffes proves that the theory is "not logically compelling nor based on fact." Holdrege asserts that the giraffe, in light of its environment, actually has a short neck in relation to its long legs. The giraffe's short neck becomes apparent when it reaches to drink from puddles, rivers, or lakes. The giraffe splays its front legs, dips its neck, and is rendered ridiculously unbalanced and susceptible to attack. If evolution has given the giraffe a long neck in order to reach food from high treetops, why not make it long enough to easily reach water to drink?

Holdrege does not offer any explanations for the length of the giraffe's neck. Instead, he urges researchers—and people in general—to further investigate the body of the giraffe and its function within the animal's given environment. Like other African animals, the giraffe faces an uncertain future unless people begin to value its role in nature. Although current giraffe populations

are considered stable, one subspecies, the Uganda or Rothschild giraffe, is endangered. There are only about 445 of them left in the wild.

Studies such as Muggenthaler's investigation of communication techniques and Holdrege's research on the giraffe's neck help make people more knowledgeable about these quiet African animals. Since giraffes cannot speak for themselves, it is up to their human admirers to advocate for their survival.

*Splaying its legs to eat grass, a giraffe illustrates just how vulnerable such a position makes it.*

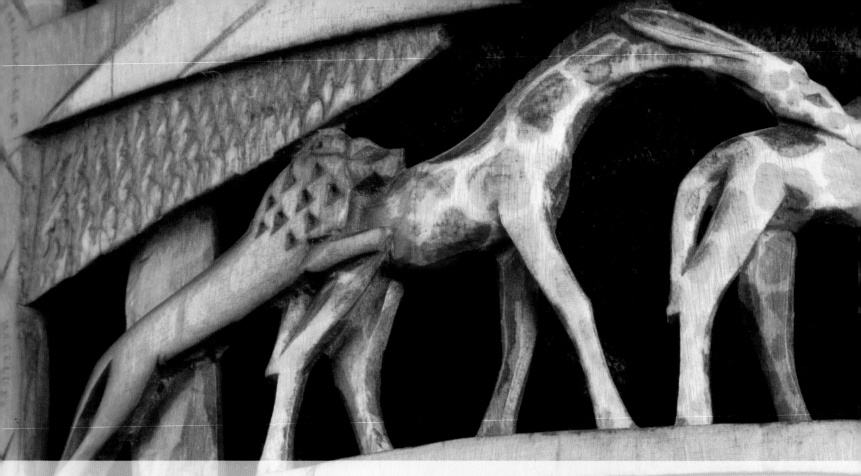

## ANIMAL TALE: WHY THE GIRAFFE CANNOT SPEAK

**The giraffe is the national emblem of Tanzania, a country in Africa. A story about the silence of the giraffe is sometimes told there to teach children that listening and observing are often more important than speaking. The story takes place at the beginning of the world, shortly after the creation of all the animals.**

---

After the Great Creator had made all the animals, he gave to each animal one wish.

"Think hard, animals of the plains," he said. "Each of you will be given one gift by the grace of my hand. Choose wisely, for you will receive only one gift."

The lion shook his great mane and rippled his massive muscles. None of the other animals seemed to notice. The lion said to himself, "These other animals have no idea how strong I am. I shall ask for a noble voice so that all will respect me." He walked forward and made his request.

"Very well," said the Creator. "Here is your roar."

The lion opened his mouth, and an immense, ground-shaking growl could be heard for miles around. The cheetah heard the loud roar of the lion and was afraid. "I must be fast," he thought, "so that I can outrun the terrible lion."

"Very well," said the Creator. "Here is a long body and quick legs for running."

The cheetah stretched his body and took off in a quick sprint. The hyena heard the lion and saw the quickness of the cheetah. He wondered how he would compete for food with such animals. "I will ask for a large pack," he thought. "That way, we can work together to communicate and catch food."

"Very well," said the Great Creator. "Here is a large pack, and each of you has a chirping voice so that you can talk to one another."

The monkey heard the great roar of the lion, saw the quick speed of the cheetah, and the great numbers of hyenas. "I must ask for long arms and clinging hands and feet so that I can climb the trees and escape these great hunters."

"Very well," said the Great Creator. "Here are long arms. Here are your hands with wide palms and long fingers for holding branches." The monkey scampered to the nearest tree and climbed up to the very top. He twittered with glee.

The elephant heard the great roar of the lion, saw the quick speed of the cheetah, the great numbers of hyenas, and the climbing arms and legs of the monkey. He thought, "I must ask for a long life

and good memory so that I can preserve my kind."

"Very well," said the Great Creator. "You will live long and remember all things."

When the creator turned to the giraffe, he said, "And what gift do you wish for yourself, Giraffe?"

The giraffe thought for a long while. Then he said, "Great Creator, it is my wish to have wisdom."

"Well spoken," said the Great Creator. "Talkative people are fools, but silence is wisdom."

The giraffe looked at the Great Creator but said nothing. The Great Creator touched the head of the giraffe. "You will never speak, Giraffe, so that all will understand your wisdom."

That is why giraffes, even today, see and hear everything, but never make a sound.

## GLOSSARY

**camouflaging** – hiding, due to coloring or markings that blend in with a given environment

**cartilage** – the firm, flexible connective tissue attached to bones

**coronation** – the ceremony of crowning a king or queen

**decimated** – destroyed a great number or proportion of something

**evolution** – the process of adapting to survive in a certain environment

**extinction** – the act or process of becoming extinct; coming to an end or dying out

**foraging** – wandering around an area in search of food

**gait** – a manner of walking, stepping, or running

**habitat** – the natural environment of an animal

**naturalists** – people who study plants and animals in their natural surroundings

**neck** – to use the neck to fight

**parasites** – organisms that live on or in the body of another animal

**predators** – animals that live by preying on other animals

**pride** – a group of lions

**regurgitated** – the partially digested food brought back up from an animal's stomach

**ruminants** – hoofed, even-toed, horned mammals, such as cattle, sheep, goats, deer, and giraffes, whose stomachs are divided into four compartments and that chew a cud

**savanna** – a plain characterized by coarse grasses and scattered tree growth, as in eastern Africa

**spar** – to fight with an opponent

**submission** – the act or instance of submitting, or surrendering power to another

**suckle** – to nurse at the breast or udder of a female mammal

**vegetation** – all the plants or plant life of a place

**vertebrae** – the bones of the spinal column that run from the mammal's neck down its back

## SELECTED BIBLIOGRAPHY

Dagg, A. I., and J. B. Foster. *The Giraffe: Its Biology, Behavior, and Ecology.* New York: Van Nostrand Reinhold, 1976.

Holdrege, Craig. "The Giraffe's Short Neck." The Nature Institute. http://natureinstitute.org/pub/ic/ic10/giraffe.htm.

Milton, Nancy. *The Giraffe That Walked to Paris.* New York: Random House, 1994.

Nature. "Tall Blondes: Silent Sentinels?" Public Broadcasting System. http://www.pbs.org/wnet/nature/tallblondes/infrasound.html.

Schlein, Miriam. *The Silent Giant.* New York: Four Winds Press, 1976.

Sherr, Lynn. *Tall Blondes: A Book about Giraffes.* Kansas City, Mo.: Andrews McMeel Publishing, 1997.

*From the time a giraffe is born it sports a pair of horns, which are hairier when it is young.*

# INDEX